United States Government Accountability Office

Testimony

Before the Subcommittee on Oversight and Management Efficiency, Committee on Homeland Security, House of Representatives

For Release on Delivery
Expected at 9:00 a.m. EST
Friday, April 26, 2013

DEPARTMENT OF HOMELAND SECURITY

Opportunities Exist to Strengthen Efficiency and Effectiveness, Achieve Cost Savings, and Improve Management Functions

Statement of Cathleen A. Berrick, Managing Director
Homeland Security and Justice

I0448681

April 2013

GAO

Accountability * Integrity * Reliability

Highlights

Highlights of GAO-13-547T, a testimony before the Subcommittee on Oversight and Management Efficiency, Committee on Homeland Security, House of Representatives

DEPARTMENT OF HOMELAND SECURITY

Opportunities Exist to Strengthen Efficiency and Effectiveness, Achieve Cost Savings, and Improve Management Functions

Why GAO Did This Study

Since beginning operations in 2003, DHS has become the third-largest federal department, with more than 224,000 employees and an annual budget of about $60 billion. Over the past 10 years, DHS has implemented key homeland security operations and achieved important goals to create and strengthen a foundation to reach its potential. Since 2003, GAO has issued more than 1,300 reports and congressional testimonies designed to strengthen DHS's program management, performance measurement efforts, and management processes, among other things. GAO has reported that overlap and fragmentation among government programs, including those of DHS, can cause potential duplication, and reducing it could save billions of tax dollars annually and help agencies provide more efficient and effective services. Moreover, in 2003, GAO designated implementing and transforming DHS as high risk because it had to transform 22 agencies into one department, and failure to address associated risks could have serious consequences. This statement addresses (1) opportunities for DHS to reduce fragmentation, overlap, and duplication in its programs; save tax dollars; and enhance revenue, and (2) opportunities for DHS to strengthen its management functions.

What GAO Recommends

While this testimony contains no new recommendations, GAO previously made about 1,800 recommendations to DHS designed to strengthen its programs and operations. The department has implemented more than 60 percent of them and has actions under way to address others.

View GAO-13-547T. For more information, contact Cathleen A. Berrick at (202) 512-3404 or berrickc@gao.gov.

What GAO Found

Since 2011, GAO has identified 11 areas across the Department of Homeland Security (DHS) where fragmentation, overlap, or potential duplication exists and 13 areas of opportunity for cost savings or enhanced revenue collections. In these reports, GAO has suggested 53 total actions to the department and Congress to help strengthen the efficiency and effectiveness of DHS operations. In GAO's 2013 annual report on federal programs, agencies, offices, and initiatives that have duplicative goals or activities, GAO identified 6 new areas where DHS could take actions to address fragmentation, overlap, or potential duplication or achieve significant cost savings. For example, GAO found that DHS does not have a department-wide policy defining research and development (R&D) or guidance directing components how to report R&D activities. Thus, DHS does not know its total annual investment in R&D, which limits its ability to oversee components' R&D efforts. In particular, GAO identified at least 6 components with R&D activities and an additional $255 million in R&D obligations in fiscal year 2011 by DHS components that was not centrally tracked. GAO suggested that DHS develop and implement policies and guidance for defining and overseeing R&D at the department. In addition, GAO reported that by reviewing the appropriateness of the federal cost share the Transportation Security Administration (TSA) applies to agreements financing airport facility modification projects related to the installation of checked baggage screening systems, TSA could, if a reduced cost share was deemed appropriate, achieve cost efficiencies of up to $300 million by 2030 and be positioned to install a greater number of optimal baggage screening systems. GAO has also updated its assessments of the progress that DHS and Congress have made in addressing the suggested actions from the 2011 and 2012 annual reports. As of March 2013, of the 42 actions from these reports, 5 have been addressed (12 percent), 24 have been partially addressed (57 percent), and the remaining 13 have not been addressed (31 percent). Although DHS and Congress have made some progress in addressing the issues that GAO has previously identified, additional steps are needed to address the remaining areas to achieve associated benefits.

While challenges remain across its missions, DHS has made considerable progress since 2003 in transforming its original component agencies into a single department. As a result, in its 2013 biennial high-risk update, GAO narrowed the scope of the area and changed its focus and name from *Implementing and Transforming the Department of Homeland Security* to *Strengthening the Department of Homeland Security Management Functions*. To more fully address this area, DHS needs to further strengthen its acquisition, information technology, and financial and human capital management functions. Of the 31 actions and outcomes GAO identified as important to addressing this area, DHS has fully or mostly addressed 8, partially addressed 16, and initiated 7. Moving forward, DHS needs to, for example, validate required acquisition documents in a timely manner, and demonstrate measurable progress in meeting cost, schedule, and performance metrics for its major acquisition programs. In addition, DHS has begun to implement a governance structure to improve information technology management consistent with best practices, but the structure covers less than 20 percent of DHS's major information technology investments.

_____ United States Government Accountability Office

Chairman Duncan, Ranking Member Barber, and Members of the Subcommittee:

I am pleased to be here today to discuss our work on opportunities for the Department of Homeland Security (DHS) to eliminate fragmentation, overlap, and duplication in its programs; enhance revenue; and improve management functions at the department.[1] Since beginning operations in 2003, DHS has become the third-largest federal department, with more than 224,000 employees and an annual budget of about $60 billion. Over the past 10 years, DHS has implemented key homeland security operations and achieved important goals to create and strengthen a foundation to reach its potential. Since 2003, we have made approximately 1,800 recommendations to DHS across more than 1,300 reports and congressional testimonies designed to strengthen program management, performance-measurement efforts, and management processes, and enhance coordination and information sharing, among other things. DHS has implemented more than 60 percent of these recommendations and has actions under way to address others. However, the department has more to do to ensure that it conducts its missions efficiently and effectively while simultaneously preparing to address future challenges that face the department and the nation.

On April 9, 2013, we issued our third report in response to the statutory requirement that we identify and report annually on federal programs, agencies, offices and initiatives that have duplicative goals or activities.[2] Since 2011, we have identified 162 areas across the federal government where Congress or executive branch agencies, including DHS, could take action to reduce fragmentation, overlap, and duplication or achieve cost

---

[1]Fragmentation refers to those circumstances in which more than one federal agency (or more than one organization within an agency) is involved in the same broad area of national need and opportunities exist to improve service delivery. Overlap occurs when multiple agencies or programs have similar goals, engage in similar activities or strategies to achieve them, or target similar beneficiaries. Duplication occurs when two or more agencies or programs are engaged in the same activities or provide the same services to the same beneficiaries.

[2]Pub. L. No. 111-139, § 21, 124 Stat. 8, 29-30 (2010), 31 U.S.C. § 712 note.

savings to address the rapidly building fiscal pressures facing our nation.[3] We reported that fragmentation among government programs or activities can be a harbinger of potential overlap or duplication. Reducing or eliminating fragmentation, overlap, or duplication could potentially save billions of tax dollars annually and help agencies provide more efficient and effective services.

Moreover, in February 2013, we reported on DHS's efforts to address the high-risk area of Strengthening the Department of Homeland Security Management Functions.[4] We first designated this area as high-risk in 2003 because DHS had to consolidate 22 agencies—several with major management challenges—into one department. Further, failure to effectively address DHS's management and mission risks could have serious consequences for U.S. national and economic security.

My statement today is based on these reports and addresses (1) opportunities for DHS to reduce fragmentation, overlap, and duplication in its programs; save tax dollars; and enhance revenue, and (2) opportunities for DHS to strengthen its management functions. For these past reports, among other things, we analyzed DHS documents, reviewed and updated our past reports issued since DHS began its operations in March 2003, and, interviewed DHS officials. More detailed information on the scope and methodology of our previous work can be found within each specific report. We conducted this work in accordance with generally accepted government auditing standards.

---

[3] GAO, *Opportunities to Reduce Potential Duplication in Government Programs, Save Tax Dollars, and Enhance Revenue*, GAO-11-318SP (Washington, D.C.: Mar. 1, 2011); *2012 Annual Report: Opportunities to Reduce Duplication, Overlap and Fragmentation, Achieve Savings, and Enhance Revenue*, GAO-12-342SP (Washington D.C.: Feb. 28, 2012); and *2013 Annual Report: Actions Needed to Reduce Fragmentation, Overlap, and Duplication and Achieve Other Financial Benefits*, GAO-13-279SP (Washington, D.C.: Apr. 9, 2013).

[4] GAO, *High-Risk Series: An Update*, GAO-13-283 (Washington, D.C.: February 2013).

DHS Can Strengthen the Efficiency and Effectiveness of Its Operations and Achieve Cost Savings by Reducing Fragmented, Overlapping, or Potentially Duplicative Activities

Areas of Fragmentation, Overlap, and Potential Duplication at DHS

Since 2011, we have identified 11 areas across DHS where fragmentation, overlap, or potential duplication exists, and suggested 24 actions to the department and Congress to help strengthen the efficiency and effectiveness of DHS operations.[5] In some cases, there is sufficient information available to show that if actions are taken to address individual issues, significant financial benefits may be realized. In other cases, precise estimates of the extent of potential unnecessary duplication, and the cost savings that can be achieved by eliminating any such duplication, are difficult to specify in advance of congressional and executive branch decision making. However, given the range of areas we identified at DHS and the magnitude of many of the programs, the cost savings associated with addressing these issues could be significant.

In April 2013, we identified 2 new areas where DHS could take actions to address fragmentation, overlap, or potential duplication.[6] First, we found that DHS does not have a department-wide policy defining research and development (R&D) or guidance directing how components are to report

---

[5]In many cases, the existence of fragmentation, overlap, or duplication can be difficult to determine precisely because of a lack of data on programs and activities. Where information was not available that would have provided conclusive evidence of fragmentation, overlap, or duplication, we often refer to potential unnecessary duplication.

[6]GAO-13-279SP.

R&D activities. As a result, the department does not know its total annual investment in R&D, a fact that limits DHS's ability to oversee components' R&D efforts and align them with agency-wide R&D goals and priorities. DHS's Science and Technology Directorate, Domestic Nuclear Detection Office, and the U.S. Coast Guard—the only DHS components that report R&D-related budget authority to the Office of Management and Budget (OMB) as part of the budget process—reported $568 million in fiscal year 2011 R&D budget authority. However, we identified at least 6 components with R&D activities and an additional $255 million in R&D obligations in fiscal year 2011 by other DHS components that were not reported to OMB in the budget process. To address this issue, we suggested that DHS develop and implement policies and guidance for defining and overseeing R&D at the department. Second, we reported that the fragmentation of field-based information sharing can be disadvantageous if activities are uncoordinated, as well as if opportunities to leverage resources across entities are not fully exploited. We suggested that DHS and other relevant agencies develop a mechanism that will allow them to hold field-based information-sharing entities accountable for coordinating with each other and monitor and evaluate the coordination results achieved, as well as identify characteristics of entities and assess specific geographic areas in which practices that could enhance coordination and reduce unnecessary overlap could be adopted. DHS generally agreed with our suggestions and is reported taking steps to address them. Moving forward, we will monitor DHS's progress to address these actions.

Concurrent with the release of our 2013 annual report, we updated our assessments of the progress that DHS has made in addressing the actions we suggested in our 2011 and 2012 annual reports.[7] Table 1 outlines the 2011-2012 DHS-related areas in which we identified

---

[7]An area may comprise a single or multiple suggested actions. We evaluated the progress of those areas identified in our March 2011 and February 2012 reports by determining an "overall assessment" rating for each area based on the individual rating of each action with the area. For congressional actions, we applied the following criteria: "addressed" means relevant legislation has been enacted; "partially addressed" means a relevant bill has passed a committee, the House of Representatives, or the Senate, or relevant legislation only addressed part of the action needed; and "not addressed" means a bill may have been introduced but did not pass out of a committee, or no relevant legislation has been introduced. For executive branch actions, "addressed" means implementation of the action needed has been completed; "partially addressed" means a response to the action needed is in development, but not yet completed; and "not addressed" means that minimal or no progress has been made toward implementing the action needed.

fragmentation, overlap, or potential duplication, and highlights DHS's and Congress's progress in addressing them.

Table 1: Assessment of DHS's Progress in Addressing the Areas of Fragmentation, Overlap, or Duplication Identified in the 2011-2012 Annual Reports

Annual report	Areas identified[a]	Overall assessment of 2011 – 2012 actions[b]
2011	**Securing the Northern Border** (Area 22): Department of Homeland Security (DHS) oversight could help eliminate potential duplicating efforts of interagency forums in securing the northern border.	○
2011	**Transportation Security Administration (TSA) Security Assessments** (Area 24): TSA's security assessments on commercial trucking companies overlap with those of another agency, but efforts are under way to address the overlap.	◑
2011	**Sharing Security-Related Information with Public Transit Agencies** (Area 25): The Department of Homeland Security could streamline mechanisms for sharing security-related information with public transit agencies to help address overlapping information.	◑
2011	**Federal Emergency Management Agency (FEMA) Grants** (Area 26): FEMA needs to improve its oversight of grants and establish a framework for assessing capabilities to identify gaps and prioritize investments.	◑
2012	**Protection of Food and Agriculture** (Area 1): Centrally coordinated oversight is needed to ensure more than nine federal agencies effectively and efficiently implement the nation's fragmented policy to defend the food and agriculture systems against potential terrorist attacks and major disasters.	◑
2012	**Cybersecurity Human Capital** (Area 12): Government-wide initiatives to enhance the cybersecurity workforce in the federal government need better structure, planning, guidance, and coordination to reduce duplication.	◑
2012	**Homeland Security Grants** (Area 17): DHS needs better project information and coordination among four overlapping grant programs.	◑
2012	**Federal Facility Risk Assessments** (Area 18): Agencies are making duplicate payments for facility risk assessments by completing their own assessments while also paying DHS for assessments that the department is not performing.	◑
2012	**Information Technology Investment Management** (Area 19): The Office of Management and Budget and the Departments of Defense and Energy need to address potentially duplicative information technology investments to avoid investing in unnecessary systems.	◑

Legend:

◑ = Partially addressed, meaning at least one action needed in that area showed some progress toward implementation, but not all actions were addressed.

○ = Not addressed, meaning none of the actions needed in that area were addressed.

Source: GAO.

[a]The area numbers indicate the number assigned to the area when it was originally reported.

[b]Assessment as of March 6, 2013.

In our March 2011 and February 2012 reports, in particular, we suggested that DHS or Congress take 21 actions to address the areas of overlap or potential duplication that we found. Of these 21 actions, 2 (approximately 10 percent) have been addressed, 13 (approximately 62 percent) have been partially addressed, and the remaining 6 (approximately 29 percent) have not been addressed.[8] For example, to address the potential for overlap among three information-sharing mechanisms that DHS funds and uses to communicate security-related information with public transit agencies, in March 2011, we suggested that DHS could identify and implement ways to more efficiently share security-related information by assessing the various mechanisms available to public transit agencies.[9] We assessed this action as partially addressed because TSA has taken steps to streamline information sharing with public transit agencies, but the agency continues to maintain various mechanisms to share such information. In March 2011, we also found that TSA's security assessments for hazardous material trucking companies overlapped with efforts conducted by the Department of Transportation's (DOT) Federal Motor Carrier Safety Administration (FMCSA), and as a result, government resources were not being used effectively. After we discussed this overlap with TSA in January 2011, agency officials stated that, moving forward, they intend to only conduct reviews on trucking companies that are not covered by FMCSA's program, an action that, if implemented as intended, we projected could save more than $1 million over the next 5 years. We also suggested that TSA and FMCSA could share each other's schedules for conducting future security reviews, and avoid scheduling reviews on hazardous material trucking companies that have recently received, or are scheduled to receive, a review from the other agency. We assessed this action as addressed because in August 2011, TSA reported that it had discontinued conducting security reviews on trucking companies that are covered by the FMCSA program. Discontinuing such reviews should eliminate the short-term overlap between TSA's and FMCSA's reviews of hazardous material trucking companies.

Although the executive branch and Congress have made some progress in addressing the issues that we have previously identified, additional

---

[8]Percentages do not add to 100 percent because of rounding.

[9]DHS could not provide us with a reliable estimate of the potential cost savings resulting from consolidating these three mechanisms.

steps are needed to address the remaining areas and achieve associated benefits. For example, to eliminate potential duplicating efforts of interagency forums in securing the northern border, in March 2011, we reported that DHS should provide guidance to and oversight of interagency forums to prevent duplication of efforts and help effectively utilize personnel resources to strengthen coordination efforts along the northern border.[10] Further, the four DHS grant programs that we reported on in February 2012—the State Homeland Security Program, the Urban Areas Security Initiative, the Port Security Grant Program, and the Transit Security Grant Program—have multiple areas of overlap and can be sources of potential unnecessary duplication. These grant programs, which FEMA used to allocate about $20.3 billion to grant recipients from fiscal years 2002 through 2011, have similar goals and fund similar activities, such as equipment and training, in overlapping jurisdictions. To address these areas of overlap, we reported that Congress may want to consider requiring DHS to report on the results of its efforts to identify and prevent unnecessary duplication within and across these grant programs, and consider these results when making future funding decisions for these programs. Such reporting could help ensure that both Congress and FEMA steer scarce resources to homeland security needs in the most efficient, cost-effective way possible.[11] See appendix I, table 4, for a summary of the fragmentation, overlap, and duplication areas and actions we identified in our 2011-2013 annual reports that are relevant to DHS.

---

[10]As of March 2013, DHS had not taken steps to determine the benefits of participating in the interagency forums or identified the costs incurred by all partners participating in each forum.

[11]The President's fiscal year 2014 budget request proposes consolidating state and local preparedness grant programs (excluding Emergency Management Performance Grants and fire grants) into the National Preparedness Grant Program. If approved, and depending on its final form and execution, the consolidated National Preparedness Grant Program could help reduce redundancies and mitigate the potential for unnecessary duplication.

Opportunities for Cost-Saving and Revenue Enhancements at DHS

Our 2011-2013 annual reports also identified 13 areas where DHS or Congress should consider taking 29 actions to reduce the cost of operations or enhance revenue collection for the Department of the Treasury.[12] Most recently, in April 2013, we identified 4 cost-savings and revenue enhancement areas related to DHS. Table 2 provides a summary of the 2011-2012 DHS-related areas in which we identified opportunities for cost savings or revenue enhancement, as well the status of efforts to address these areas.

Table 2: Cost Savings and Revenue Enhancement Opportunities Identified in Our 2013 Annual Report

Annual report	Areas identified[a]
2013	**Agricultural Quarantine Inspection Fees** (Area 18): The United States Department of Agriculture's Animal and Plant Health Inspection Service could have achieved as much as $325 million in savings (based on fiscal year 2011 data, as reported in GAO's March 2013 report) by more fully aligning fees with program costs; although the savings would be recurring, the amount would depend on the cost-collections gap in a given fiscal year and would result in a reduced reliance on U.S. Customs and Border Protection's annual Salaries and Expenses appropriations used for agricultural inspection services.
2013	**Checked Baggage Screening** (Area 28): By reviewing the appropriateness of the federal cost share the Transportation Security Administration applies to agreements financing airport facility modification projects related to the installation of checked baggage screening systems, the Transportation Security Administration could, if a reduced cost share was deemed appropriate, achieve cost efficiencies of up to $300 million by 2030 and be positioned to install a greater number of optimal baggage screening systems than it currently anticipates.
2013	**Cloud Computing** (Area 29): Better planning of cloud-based computing solutions provides opportunity for potential savings of millions of dollars.
2013	**Information Technology Operations and Maintenance** (Area 30): Strengthening oversight of key federal agencies' major information technology investments in operations and maintenance provides opportunity for savings on billions in information technology investments.

Source: GAO.

[a]The area numbers indicate the number assigned to the area when it was originally reported.

In addition, in April 2013 we also reported on the steps that DHS and Congress have taken to address the cost savings and revenue enhancement areas identified in our 2011 and 2012 annual reports. Table 3 provides a summary of the 2011-2012 DHS-related areas in which we

---

[12]In some cases, there is sufficient information to estimate potential savings or other benefits if actions are taken to address individual issues. In other cases, estimates of cost savings or other benefits would depend upon what congressional and executive branch decisions were made, including how certain our recommendations are implemented. See appendix I, table 5, for a summary of cost savings and revenue enhancement areas and actions we identified in our 2011-2013 annual reports that are relevant to DHS.

identified opportunities for cost savings or revenue enhancement, as well the status of efforts to address these areas.

Table 3: Assessments of DHS's Progress in Addressing the Areas of Cost Savings or Revenue Enhancement in the 2011-2012 Annual Reports

Annual report	Areas identified[a]	Overall assessment of 2011 – 2012 actions[b]
2011	**Award Fee Contracts** (Area 49): Adherence to guidance on award fee contracts could improve agencies' use of award fees and produce savings. Several major agencies spent over $300 billion from fiscal year 2004 through fiscal year 2008 on contracts that included monetary incentives known as award fees.	●
2011	**DHS's Management of Acquisitions** (Area 75/76): The Department of Homeland Security's (DHS) management of acquisitions could be strengthened to reduce inefficiencies, cost overruns, and schedule and performance shortfalls. DHS acquisition spending increased by 66 percent since fiscal year 2004—$8.5 billion in fiscal year 2004 to $14.2 billion in fiscal year 2009.	◐
2011	**TSA's Behavior-Based Screening** (Area 77): Validation of the Transportation Security Administration's (TSA) behavior-based screening program is needed to justify funding or expansion.	◐
2011	**Baggage Screening Systems** (Area 78): More efficient baggage screening systems could result in about $470 million in reduced TSA personnel costs over the next 5 years.	◐
2011	**Customs Fee Collections** (Area 79): Clarifying availability of certain customs fee collections could produce a one-time savings of $640 million.	●
2012	**Border Security** (Area 47): Delaying proposed investments for future acquisitions of border surveillance technology until DHS better defines and measures benefits and estimates life-cycle costs could help ensure the most effective use of future program funding. U.S. Customs and Border Protection (CBP) requested $242 million to fund the new plan for fiscal year 2012.	◐
2012	**Passenger Aviation Security Fees** (Area 48): Options for adjusting the passenger aviation security fee could further offset billions of dollars in civil aviation security costs. These options could increase fee collections from about $2 billion to $10 billion over 5 years.	○
2012	**Immigration Inspection Fee** (Area 49): The air passenger immigration inspection user fee should be reviewed and adjusted to fully recover the cost of the air passenger immigration inspection activities conducted by DHS's U.S. Immigration and Customs Enforcement and CBP rather than using general fund appropriations. In 2011. This could have resulted in a reduction of about $178 million in appropriated funds used for inspection services.	◐
2012	**Domestic Disaster Assistance** (Area 51): The Federal Emergency Management Agency could reduce the costs to the federal government related to major disasters declared by the President by updating the principal indicator on which disaster funding decisions are based and better measuring a state's capacity to respond without federal assistance.	○

Legend:

● = Addressed, meaning all actions needed in that area were addressed.

◐ = Partially addressed, meaning at least one action needed in that area showed some progress toward implementation, but not all actions were addressed.

○ = Not addressed, meaning none of the actions needed in that area were addressed.

Source: GAO

^aThe area numbers indicate the number assigned to the area when it was originally reported.

^bAssessment as of March 6, 2013.

Of the 21 related actions we suggested that DHS or Congress take in our March 2011 and February 2012 reports to either reduce the cost of government operations or enhance revenue collection, as of March 2013, 3 (about 14 percent) have been addressed, 11 (about 52 percent) have been partially addressed, and 7 (about 33 percent) have not been addressed.[13] For example, in February 2012, we reported that to increase the likelihood of successful implementation of the Arizona Border Surveillance Technology Plan, minimize performance risks and help justify program funding, the Commissioner of CBP should update the agency's cost estimate for the plan using best practices. This year, we assessed this action as partially addressed because CBP initiated action to update its cost estimate, using best practices, for the plan by providing revised cost estimates in February and March 2012 for the plan's two largest projects. However, CBP has not independently verified its life cycle cost estimates for these projects with independent cost estimates and reconciled any differences with each system's respective life cycle cost estimate, consistent with best practices. Such action would help CBP better ensure the reliability of each system's cost estimate. Further, in March 2011, we stated that Congress may wish to consider limiting program funding pending receipt of an independent assessment of TSA's Screening of Passengers by Observation Techniques (SPOT) program. This year, we assessed this action as addressed because Congress froze the program funds at the fiscal year 2010 level and funded less than half of TSA's fiscal year 2012 request for full-time behavior detection officers.

Although DHS and Congress have made some progress in addressing the issues that we have previously identified that may produce cost savings or revenue enhancements, additional steps are needed. For example, in February 2012, we reported that FEMA should develop and implement a methodology that provides a more comprehensive assessment of a jurisdiction's capability to respond to and recover from a

---

[13]Percentages do not add to 100 percent because of rounding. In assessing progress on the areas we identified in our 2011 annual report for this year's report, we combined two areas related to the Department of Homeland Security's management of acquisitions (Areas 75 and 76) into one area.

disaster without federal assistance. As of March 2013, FEMA had not addressed this action. In addition, in the 2012 report, we suggested that Congress, working with the Administrator of TSA, may wish to consider increasing the passenger aviation security fee according to one of many options, including but not limited to the President's Deficit Reduction Plan option ($7.50 per one-way trip by 2017) or the Congressional Budget Office, President's Debt Commission, and House Budget Committee options ($5 per one-way trip). These options could increase fee collections over existing levels from about $2 billion to $10 billion over 5 years. However, as of March 2013, Congress had not passed legislation to increase the passenger security fee.[14] For additional information on our assessment of DHS's and Congress's efforts to address our previously reported actions, see *GAO's Action Tracker*.[15]

DHS Needs to Strengthen Its Management Functions

Following its establishment in 2003, DHS focused its efforts primarily on implementing its various missions to meet pressing homeland security needs and threats, and less on creating and integrating a fully and effectively functioning department. As the department matured, it has put into place management policies and processes and made a range of other enhancements to its management functions, which include acquisition, information technology, financial, and human capital management. However, DHS has not always effectively executed or integrated these functions.

---

[14]In the President's fiscal year 2014 budget request, TSA proposes to replace the current "per-enplanement" fee structure with a "per one-way trip" fee structure so that passengers pay the fee only one time when traveling to their destination. It also removes the current statutory fee limit and replaces it with a statutory fee minimum of $5.00 in 2014, with annual incremental increases of 50 cents from 2015 to 2019, resulting in a fee of $7.50 per one-way trip in 2019 and thereafter. According to TSA, the proposed fee would increase collections by an estimated $25.9 billion over 10 years. Of this amount, $7.9 billion will be applied to increase offsets to the discretionary costs of aviation security and the remaining $18 billion will be treated a mandatory savings and deposited in the general fund for deficit reduction. This proposal presents an option that, consistent with our suggested action, Congress may consider in determining whether to take legislative action to change the fee.

[15]*GAO's Action Tracker* is a publicly accessible website of the 162 areas and approximately 380 suggested actions presented in our 2011, 2012, and 2013 reports. *GAO's Action Tracker* includes progress updates and assessments of legislative and executive branch actions needed. We will add areas and suggested actions identified in future reports to *GAO's Action Tracker* and periodically update the status of all identified areas and activities.

The department has made considerable progress in transforming its original component agencies into a single cabinet-level department and positioning itself to achieve its full potential; however, challenges remain for DHS to address across its range of missions. DHS has also made important strides in strengthening the department's management functions and in integrating those functions across the department. As a result, in February 2013, we narrowed the scope of the high-risk area and changed the focus and name from *Implementing and Transforming the Department of Homeland Security* to *Strengthening the Department of Homeland Security Management Functions*.[16] Of the 31 actions and outcomes GAO identified as important to addressing this area, DHS has fully or mostly addressed 8, partially addressed 16, and initiated 7. Moving forward, continued progress is needed in order to mitigate the risks that management weaknesses pose to mission accomplishment and the efficient and effective use of the department's resources. For example:

- **Acquisition management**: Although DHS has made progress in strengthening its acquisition function, most of DHS's major acquisition programs continue to cost more than expected, take longer to deploy than planned, or deliver less capability than promised. We identified 42 programs that experienced cost growth, schedule slips, or both, with 16 of the programs' costs increasing from a total of $19.7 billion in 2008 to $52.2 billion in 2011—an aggregate increase of 166 percent. We reported in September 2012 that DHS leadership has authorized and continued to invest in major acquisition programs even though the vast majority of those programs lack foundational documents demonstrating the knowledge needed to help manage risks and measure performance.[17] We recommended that DHS modify acquisition policy to better reflect key program and portfolio management practices and ensure acquisition programs fully comply with DHS acquisition policy. DHS concurred with our recommendations and reported taking actions to address some of them. Moving forward, DHS needs to, for example, validate required acquisition documents in a timely manner, and demonstrate measurable progress in meeting cost, schedule, and performance metrics for its major acquisition programs.

---

[16]GAO-13-283.

[17]GAO, *Homeland Security: DHS Requires More Disciplined Investment Management to Help Meet Mission Needs*, GAO-12-833, (Washington D.C.: Sept. 18, 2012).

- **Information technology management:** DHS has defined and begun to implement a vision for a tiered governance structure intended to improve information technology (IT) program and portfolio management, which is generally consistent with best practices. However, the governance structure covers less than 20 percent (about 16 of 80) of DHS's major IT investments and 3 of its 13 portfolios, and the department has not yet finalized the policies and procedures associated with this structure. In July 2012, we recommended that DHS finalize the policies and procedures and continue to implement the structure. DHS agreed with these recommendations and estimated it would address them by September 2013.[18]

- **Financial management:** DHS has, among other things, received a qualified audit opinion on its fiscal year 2012 financial statements for the first time since the department's creation. DHS is working to resolve the audit qualification to obtain an unqualified opinion for fiscal year 2013. However, DHS components are currently in the early planning stages of their financial systems modernization efforts, and until these efforts are complete, their current systems will continue to inadequately support effective financial management, in part because of their lack of substantial compliance with key federal financial management requirements. Without sound controls and systems, DHS faces challenges in obtaining and sustaining audit opinions on its financial statement and internal controls over financial reporting, as well as ensuring its financial management systems generate reliable, useful, and timely information for day-to-day decision making.

- **Human capital management:** In December 2012, we identified several factors that have hampered DHS's strategic workforce planning efforts and recommended, among other things, that DHS identify and document additional performance measures to assess workforce planning efforts.[19] DHS agreed with these recommendations and stated that it plans to take actions to address them. In addition, DHS has made efforts to improve employee morale, such as taking actions to determine the root causes of morale

---

[18]GAO, *Information Technology: DHS Needs to Further Define and Implement Its New Governance Process*, GAO-12-818 (Washington, D.C.: July 25, 2012).

[19]GAO, *DHS Strategic Workforce Planning: Oversight of Departmentwide Efforts Should Be Strengthened*, GAO-13-65 (Washington D.C.: Dec. 3, 2012).

problems. Despite these efforts, however, federal surveys have consistently found that DHS employees are less satisfied with their jobs than the government-wide average. In September 2012, we recommended, among other things, that DHS improve its root cause analysis efforts of morale issues. DHS agreed with these recommendations and noted actions it plans to take to address them.[20]

In conclusion, given DHS's significant leadership responsibilities in securing the homeland, it is critical that the department's programs and activities are operating as efficiently and effectively as possible; that they are sustainable; and that they continue to mature, evolve, and adapt to address pressing security needs. Since it began operations in 2003, DHS has implemented key homeland security operations and achieved important goals and milestones in many areas. These accomplishments are especially noteworthy given that the department has had to work to transform itself into a fully functioning cabinet department while implementing its missions. However, our work has shown that DHS can take actions to reduce fragmentation, overlap, and unnecessary duplication to improve the efficiency of its operations and achieve cost savings in several areas. Further, DHS has taken steps to strengthen its management functions and integrate them across the department; however, continued progress is needed to mitigate the risks that management weaknesses pose to mission accomplishment and the efficient and effective use of the department's resources. DHS has indeed made significant strides in protecting the homeland, but has yet to reach its full potential.

Chairman Duncan, Ranking Member Barber, and members of the subcommittee, this concludes my prepared statement. I would be pleased to respond to any questions that members of the subcommittee may have.

---

[20]GAO, *Department of Homeland Security: Taking Further Action to Better Determine Causes of Morale Problems Would Assist in Targeting Action Plans*, GAO-12-940 (Washington, D.C.: Sept. 28, 2012).

Contacts and Acknowledgments

For further information regarding this testimony, please contact Cathleen A. Berrick at (202) 512-3404 or berrickc@gao.gov. In addition, contact points for our Offices of Congressional Relations and Public Affairs may be found on the last page of this statement. Individuals who made key contributions to this testimony are Kathryn Bernet, Assistant Director; Elizabeth Luke; and Meg Ullengren.

Appendix I: Areas and Actions Identified in 2011-2013 Annual Reports Related to the Department of Homeland Security

This enclosure presents a summary of the areas and actions we identified in our 2011-2013 annual reports that are relevant to the Department of Homeland Security (DHS).[1] It also includes our assessment of the overall progress made in each of the areas and the progress made on each action that we identified in our 2011 and 2012 annual reports in which Congress and DHS could take actions to reduce or eliminate fragmentation, overlap, and potential duplication or achieve other potential financial benefits. As of April 26, 2013, we have not assessed DHS's progress in addressing the relevant 2013 areas. Table 4 presents our assessment of the overall progress made in implementing the actions needed in the areas related to fragmentation, overlap, or duplication. Table 5 presents our assessment of the overall progress made in implementing the actions needed in the areas related to cost savings or revenue enhancement.

Table 4: Assessment of DHS's Progress in Addressing the Areas of Fragmentation, Overlap, and Duplication and Related Actions Identified in 2011-2013 Annual Reports

Annual report	Areas identified	Assessment
2011	**Securing the Northern Border** (Area 22): Department of Homeland Security (DHS) oversight could help eliminate potential duplicating efforts of interagency forums in securing the northern border.	○
	Action 1: DHS should provide guidance and oversight for interagency forums— which include both Integrated Border Enforcement Team (IBET) and Border Enforcement Security Task Force (BEST) interagency forums—to help prevent duplication of effort and help efficiently utilize personnel resources to strengthen DHS's coordination efforts along the northern border.	○
	Action 2: As DHS establishes a mechanism for determining the benefits of participating in the IBET and BEST interagency forums, DHS could lead efforts to develop a framework for identifying the costs incurred by all partners participating in each forum.	○
2011	**TSA's Security Assessments** (Area 24): The Transportation Security Administration's (TSA) security assessments on commercial trucking companies overlap with those of another agency, but efforts are underway to address the overlap.	◑

[1]GAO, *Opportunities to Reduce Potential Duplication in Government Programs, Save Tax Dollars, and Enhance Revenue*, GAO-11-318SP (Washington, D.C.: Mar. 1, 2011); *2012 Annual Report: Opportunities to Reduce Duplication, Overlap, and Fragmentation, Achieve Savings, and Enhance Revenue*, GAO-12-342SP (Washington, D.C.: Feb. 28, 2012); and *2013 Annual Report: Actions Needed to Reduce Fragmentation, Overlap, and Duplication and Achieve Other Financial Benefits*, GAO-13-279SP (Washington, D.C.: Apr. 9, 2013).

**Appendix I: Areas and Actions Identified in
2011-2013 Annual Reports Related to the
Department of Homeland Security**

Annual report	Areas identified	Assessment
	Action 1: TSA and the Federal Motor Carrier Safety Administration (FMCSA) could improve interagency coordination by sharing each other's schedules for conducting future security reviews, and avoid scheduling reviews on hazardous material trucking companies that have recently received, or are scheduled to receive, a review from the other agency. TSA could also discontinue conducting voluntary security reviews on hazardous material trucking companies, thereby enabling TSA to increase its security efforts in other areas. In August 2011, TSA reported that the agency had discontinued conducting security reviews on trucking companies that are covered by the FMCSA program. Discontinuing such reviews could save more than $1 million over the next 5 years.	◗
	Action 2: TSA could request that the full results of past FMCSA security reviews of trucking companies be provided through an existing Department of Transportation (DOT) web portal. Doing so would require cooperation from FMCSA.	○
	Action 3: TSA and FMCSA should continue efforts toward the long-term goal of TSA assuming full regulatory responsibility from FMCSA for commercial trucking security, thereby reducing fragmentation.	◐
2011	**Sharing Security-Related Information with Public Transit Agencies** (Area 25): DHS could streamline mechanisms for sharing security-related information with public transit agencies to help address overlapping information.	◐
	Action 1: DHS and TSA could identify and implement ways to more efficiently share security-related information by assessing the various mechanisms available to public transit agencies—including DHS's information network, TSA's portal on the network, and the public transit analysis center—as well as the information they provide, and identify opportunities to streamline these mechanisms. TSA officials stated in September 2010 that TSA applied $2.5 billion for fiscal years 2009 and 2010 to its portal on DHS's information network, primarily on developing and organizing data for all transportation modes.	◐
	Action 2: DHS could develop and track verifiable cost data specific to each of its information-sharing mechanisms, as part of TSA streamlining and financial management efforts. Developing such baseline cost data could assist TSA in identifying potential cost savings resulting from the consolidation of these mechanisms and provide opportunities for the agency to better allocate its information-sharing resources.	◐
2011	**FEMA Grants** (Area 26): The Federal Emergency Management Agency (FEMA) needs to improve its oversight of grants and establish a framework for assessing capabilities to identify gaps and prioritize investments.	◐
	Action 1: FEMA could benefit from examining its grant programs and coordinating its application process to eliminate or reduce redundancy among grant recipients and program purposes.	◐
	Action 2: Congress may wish to consider limiting preparedness grant funding to maintaining existing capabilities (as determined by FEMA) until FEMA completes a national preparedness assessment of capability gaps at each level based on tiered, capability-specific performance objectives to enable prioritization of grant funding. In April 2011, Congress reduced funding for FEMA preparedness grants by $875 million from the amount requested in the President's fiscal year 2011 budget. In December 2011, Congress reduced funding for FEMA preparedness grants by $1.28 billion from the amount requested in the President's fiscal year 2012 budget.	◐
	Action 3: FEMA should complete a national preparedness assessment of capability gaps at each level based on tiered, capability-specific performance objectives to enable prioritization of grant funding, and FEMA could identify the potential costs for establishing and maintaining those capabilities at each level and determine what capabilities federal agencies should provide.	◐
	Action 4: Once FEMA has completed its assessment, Congress may wish to consider limiting the use of federal preparedness grant programs to fund only projects to fill identified, validated, and documented capability gaps that may (or may not) include maintaining existing capabilities developed.	○

Appendix I: Areas and Actions Identified in
2011-2013 Annual Reports Related to the
Department of Homeland Security

Annual report	Areas identified	Assessment
2012	**Protection of Food and Agriculture** (Area 1): Centrally coordinated oversight is needed to ensure more than nine federal agencies effectively and efficiently implement the nation's fragmented policy to defend the food and agriculture systems against potential terrorist attacks and major disasters.	◑
	Action 1: To help ensure that the federal government is effectively implementing the nation's food and agriculture defense policy, the Secretary of Homeland Security should resume DHS's efforts to coordinate agencies' overall Homeland Security Presidential Directive 9 (HSPD-9) implementation efforts.	◑
2012	**Cybersecurity Human Capital** (Area 12): Governmentwide initiatives to enhance cybersecurity workforce in the federal government need better structure, planning, guidance, and coordination to reduce duplication.	◑
	Action 1: To ensure that governmentwide cybersecurity workforce initiatives are better coordinated, the Directors of the Office of Management and Budget (OMB) and the Office of Personnel Management (OPM) and the Secretaries of Commerce and Homeland Security should consolidate and align efforts to define roles, responsibilities, skills, and competencies for the federal cybersecurity workforce.	◑
	Action 2: The Secretary of Homeland Security should implement a process for tracking agency use of training, gather feedback from agencies on the training's value and opportunities for improvement, and develop a process to coordinate training offered to minimize the production and distribution of duplicative products.	◑
2012	**Homeland Security Grants** (Area 17): DHS needs better project information and coordination among four overlapping grant programs.	◑
	Action 1: To help reduce the risk of unnecessary duplication by strengthening the administration and oversight of these programs, FEMA's Administrator should take steps, when developing the Non-Disaster Grants Management system and responding to the May 2011 FEMA report recommendations on data requirements, to ensure that FEMA collects project information with the level of detail needed to better position the agency to identify any potential unnecessary duplication within and across the four grant programs, weighing any additional costs of collecting these data.	◑
	Action 2: To help reduce the risk of unnecessary duplication by strengthening the administration and oversight of these programs, FEMA Administrator should explore opportunities to enhance FEMA's internal coordination and administration of the programs in order to identify and mitigate the potential for any unnecessary duplication.	◑
	Action 3: Congress may want to consider requiring DHS to report on the results of its efforts to identify and prevent unnecessary duplication within and across the State Homeland Security Program, Urban Areas Security Initiative, Port Security Grant Program, and Transit Security Grant Program, and consider these results when making future funding decisions for these programs. From fiscal years 2002 through 2011, FEMA allocated about $20.3 billion to grant recipients through these four programs.	○
2012	**Federal Facility Risk Assessments** (Area 18): Agencies are making duplicate payments for facility risk assessments by completing their own assessments, while also paying DHS for assessments that the department is not performing.	◑

Appendix I: Areas and Actions Identified in
2011-2013 Annual Reports Related to the
Department of Homeland Security

Annual report	Areas identified	Assessment
	Action 1: To address the duplicative federal facility risk assessments conducted by multiple federal agencies, the Secretary of DHS should direct the Director of the Federal Protective Service (FPS) to develop interim solutions for completing risk assessments while addressing the Risk Assessment and Management Program's (RAMP) challenges.	
	Action 2: To address the duplicative federal facility risk assessments conducted by multiple federal agencies, the Director of FPS should make information about the estimated costs of key activities and the basis for these estimates available to affected parties to improve transparency.	
	Action 3: To address the duplicative federal facility risk assessments conducted by multiple federal agencies, DHS should work with federal agencies to determine their reasons for duplicating the activities included in FPS's risk assessments and identify measures to reduce this duplication.	
2012	**Information Technology Investment Management** (Area 19): The Office of Management and Budget and the Departments of Defense and Energy need to address potentially duplicative information technology (IT) investments to avoid investing in unnecessary systems. Identifying and consolidating potentially duplicative IT investments at the Departments of Defense and Energy could result in millions of dollars in cost savings.	
	Action 5: To better ensure the agencies avoid investing in duplicative investments the Secretaries of Defense, Energy, and Homeland Security should direct their chief information officers to correct the miscategorizations for the investments GAO identified and ensure that investments are correctly categorized in agency submissions.	
2013	**Department of Homeland Security Research and Development** (Area 7): Better policies and guidance for defining, overseeing, and coordinating research and development investments and activities would help DHS address fragmentation, overlap, and potential unnecessary duplication.	a
	Action 1: The Secretary of Homeland Security should develop and implement policies and guidance for defining and overseeing research and development (R&D) at the department to ensure that DHS effectively oversees its R&D investment and efforts and reduces fragmentation, overlap, and the risk of unnecessary duplication. Such policies and guidance could be included as an update to the department's existing acquisition directive and should include the following elements: a well-understood definition of R&D that provides reasonable assurance that reliable accounting and reporting of R&D resources and activities for internal and external use are achieved; a description of the department's process and roles and responsibilities for overseeing and coordinating R&D investments and efforts; and a mechanism to track existing R&D projects and their associated costs across the department. DHS's Science and Technology Directorate, Domestic Nuclear Detection Office, and the U.S. Coast Guard—the only DHS components that report R&D-related budget authority to OMB—reported $568 million in fiscal year 2011 budget authority. However, GAO identified an additional $255 million in R&D obligations in fiscal year 2011 by other DHS components that were not reported to OMB in the budget process.	a
2013	**Field-Based Information Sharing** (Area 8): To help reduce inefficiencies resulting from overlap in analytical and investigative support activities, the Departments of Justice and Homeland Security and the Office of National Drug Control Policy (ONDCP) could improve coordination among five types of field-based information sharing entities that may collect, process, analyze, or disseminate information in support of law enforcement and counterterrorism-related efforts—Joint Terrorism Task Forces, Field Intelligence Groups, Regional Information Sharing Systems centers, state and major urban area fusion centers, and High Intensity Drug Trafficking Areas Investigative Support Centers.	a

Appendix I: Areas and Actions Identified in
2011-2013 Annual Reports Related to the
Department of Homeland Security

Annual report	Areas identified	Assessment
	Action 1: The Secretary of Homeland Security, the Attorney General, and the Director of ONDCP should work through the Information Sharing and Access Interagency Policy Committee or otherwise collaborate to develop a mechanism that will allow them to hold field-based information-sharing entities accountable for coordinating with each other and monitor and evaluate the coordination results achieved.	[a]
	Action 2: The Secretary of Homeland Security, the Attorney General, and the Director of ONDCP should work through the Information Sharing and Access Interagency Policy Committee or otherwise collaborate to identify characteristics of entities and assess specific geographic areas in which practices that could enhance coordination and reduce unnecessary overlap, such as cross-entity participation on governance boards and collocation of entities, could be further applied, and use the results to provide recommendations or guidance to the entities on implementing these practices.	[a]

Legend:

● = Addressed, meaning all actions needed in that area were addressed.

◑= Partially addressed, meaning at least one action needed in that area showed some progress toward implementation, but not all actions were addressed.

○ = Not addressed, meaning none of the actions needed in that area were addressed

Source: GAO analysis.

[a]As of April 26, 2013, we have not assessed the 2013 areas identified.

Table 5: Assessments of DHS's Progress in Addressing the Areas of Cost Savings and Revenue Enhancements and Related Actions Identified in 2011 – 2013 Annual Reports

Annual report	Areas identified	Assessment
2011	**Award Fee Contracts** (Area 49): Adherence to guidance on award fee contracts could improve agencies' use of award fees and produce savings. Several major agencies spent over $300 billion from fiscal year 2004 through fiscal year 2008 on contracts that included monetary incentives known as award fees.	●
	Action 1: Sustained progress in the use of award fees will require that contracting agencies adhere to changes to the Federal Acquisition Regulation, which in 2009 prohibited the practices of rollover of unearned award fees and awarding fees to contractors that have performed unsatisfactorily. Further efforts are needed by agencies to identify methods to evaluate the effectiveness of award fees as a tool for improving contractor performance.	●
2011	**DHS's Management of Acquisitions** (Area 75/76): The Department of Homeland Security's (DHS) management of acquisitions could be strengthened to reduce inefficiencies, cost overruns, and schedule and performance shortfalls. DHS acquisition spending has increased by 66 percent since fiscal year 2004—$8.5 billion in fiscal year 2004 to $14.2 billion in fiscal year 2009.	◑

Appendix I: Areas and Actions Identified in
2011-2013 Annual Reports Related to the
Department of Homeland Security

Annual report	Areas identified	Assessment
	Action 1: DHS should ensure that requirements and cost estimates are well defined up front.	◑
	Action 2: DHS should establish and measure performance against department-approved baselines for major acquisition programs.	◑
	Action 3: DHS should ensure that its investment decisions are transparent and documented; budget decisions are informed by the results of acquisition reviews, including acquisition information and cost estimates; sufficient management resources are identified and aligned, such as acquisition staff, to implement oversight reviews in a timely manner; and acquisition program requirements are reviewed and validated.	◑
	Action 4: DHS could take further actions to improve its management of research and development (R&D) efforts and reduce costs in procuring and deploying programs that have not been fully tested, including rigorously testing devices using actual agency operational tactics before making decisions on acquisitions. GAO has revised this action to more clearly focus on DHS acquisition management rather than DHS R&D, which is addressed separately in GAO's April 2013 report. Specifically, GAO suggests that DHS should ensure that testing of new technologies is completed and test results are addressed before making acquisition decisions.	◑
	Action 5: DHS should conduct cost-benefit analyses as part of research, development, and testing efforts, which would help DHS and congressional decision makers better assess and prioritize investment decisions, including assessing possible program alternatives that could be more cost-effective. GAO has revised this action to more clearly focus on DHS acquisition management rather than DHS R&D, which is addressed separately in GAO's April 2013 report. Specifically, GAO suggests that DHS should take actions to help decision makers better assess and prioritize investments, including possible program alternatives that could be more cost-effective.	◑
2011	**TSA's Behavior-Based Screening** (Area 77): Validation of the Transportation Security Administration's (TSA) behavior-based screening program is needed to justify funding or expansion.	◑
	Action 2: DHS could conduct additional research to provide additional information on the extent to which the Screening of Passengers by Observation Techniques (SPOT) program can be effectively implemented in airports and to help determine the need for periodic refresher training. This action was revised to consolidate it with action 1 cited in GAO's March 2011 report. Specifically, GAO suggests that DHS use an independent panel of experts to assess the methodology of its initial validation study of the TSA behavior detection program, and conduct additional research to provide further information and assurance on the extent to which the SPOT program can be effectively implemented in airports, and to help determine the need for periodic refresher training.	◑
	Action 3: Congress may wish to consider limiting program funding pending receipt of an independent assessment of TSA's SPOT program. Specifically, Congress could consider freezing appropriation levels for the SPOT program at the 2010 level until the validation effort is complete.	●
	Action 4: Upon completion of the validation effort, Congress may also wish to consider the study's results— including the SPOT program's effectiveness in using behavior-based screening techniques to detect terrorists in the aviation environment—in making future funding decisions regarding the program. Depending on the results of DHS's validation effort and congressional action, savings over the next 5 years could total tens of millions of dollars.	○
2011	**Baggage Screening Systems** (Area 78): More efficient baggage screening systems could result in about $470 million in reduced TSA personnel costs over the next 5 years.	◑

Appendix I: Areas and Actions Identified in
2011-2013 Annual Reports Related to the
Department of Homeland Security

Annual report	Areas identified	Assessment
	Action 1: TSA might achieve savings in screening personnel costs by continuing to replace or modify older checked baggage screening systems with more efficient solutions, including in-line screening systems.	◑
2011	**Customs Fee Collections** (Area 79): Clarifying availability of certain customs fee collections could produce a one-time savings of $640 million.	●
	Action 1: Congress could clarify the purposes for which the $639.4 million in unobligated balances is available. The unobligated balances have remained in U.S. Customs and Border Protection's (CBP) Customs User Fee Account for more than 10 years.	●
2012	**Border Security** (Area 47): Delaying proposed investments for future acquisitions of border surveillance technology until DHS better defines and measures benefits and estimates life-cycle costs could help ensure the most effective use of future program funding. CBP requested $242 million to fund the new plan for fiscal year 2012.	◑
	Action 1: To increase the likelihood of successful implementation of the Arizona Border Surveillance Technology Plan, minimize performance risks associated with the new approach, help justify program funding, and increase the reliability of CBP cost estimate, the Commissioner of CBP should determine the mission benefits to be derived from implementation of the plan.	◑
	Action 2: To increase the likelihood of successful implementation of the Arizona Border Surveillance Technology Plan, minimize performance risks associated with the new approach, help justify program funding, and increase the reliability of CBP cost estimate, the Commissioner of CBP should develop and apply key attributes for metrics to assess program implementation.	◑
	Action 3: To increase the likelihood of successful implementation of the Arizona Border Surveillance Technology Plan, minimize performance risks associated with the new approach, help justify program funding, and increase the reliability of CBP's cost estimate, the Commissioner of CBP should update its cost estimate for the plan using best practices.	○
	Action 4: Congress may wish to consider limiting future program funding until CBP has more fully defined the benefits and costs of its Arizona Border Surveillance Technology Plan.	
2012	**Passenger Aviation Security Fees** (Area 48): Options for adjusting the passenger aviation security fee could further offset billions of dollars in civil aviation security costs. These options could increase fee collections from about $2 billion to $10 billion over 5 years.	○
	Action 1: To help further offset billions of dollars in the federal budget for aviation security programs and activities in outlying fiscal years, Congress, working with the Administrator of TSA, should consider increasing the passenger security fee according to one of the options GAO identified in February 2012. These include the President's Deficit Reduction Plan option ($7.50 per one-way trip by 2017); the Congressional Budget Office, President's Debt Commission, and House Budget Committee options ($5.00 per one-way trip); TSA's Fiscal Year 2012 Budget Request option ($5.50 per enplanement by 2014); as well as adjusting the fee for inflation (according to GAO analysis; this option would increase the fee to about $3.00 per enplanement). These options could increase fee collections over existing levels from about $2 billion to $10 billion over 5 years.	○
2012	**Immigration Inspection Fees** (Area 49): The air passenger immigration inspection user fee should be reviewed and adjusted to fully recover the cost of the air passenger immigration inspection activities conducted by DHS's U.S. Immigration and Customs Enforcement (ICE) and CBP rather than using general fund appropriations. In 2011 this could have resulted in a reduction of about $178 million in appropriated funds used for inspection services.	◑

Appendix I: Areas and Actions Identified in
2011-2013 Annual Reports Related to the
Department of Homeland Security

Annual report	Areas identified	Assessment
	Action 1: To determine the extent to which air passenger immigration inspection fees are aligned with the costs of inspection activities, which could enable fee adjustments to reduce reliance on general fund appropriations, Congress may wish to require the Secretary of Homeland Security to require ICE and CBP to regularly report on the total cost of air passenger immigration inspections and the amount of associated fee collections.	○
	Action 2: Congress may wish to require the Secretary of Homeland Security to adjust the fee as needed so that collections are aligned with total inspection costs, if it is determined that total immigration fee collections do not cover total immigration inspection costs. This action was revised to reflect efforts by ICE and CBP to determine the extent to which immigration fee collections cover reimbursable activities. Specifically, GAO is suggesting that Congress may wish to adjust the immigration inspection fee as needed so that collections are aligned with total inspection costs, now that ICE and CBP have determined that total immigration fee collections do not cover total immigration inspection costs.	○
	Action 3: To determine the extent to which air passenger immigration inspection fees are aligned with the costs of inspection activities, which could enable fee adjustments to reduce reliance on general fund appropriations, Congress may wish to require the Secretary of Homeland Security to direct ICE to amend its cost study methodology to determine the extent to which air passenger fee collections cover reimbursable activities.	◑
	Action 4: To determine the extent to which air passenger immigration inspection fees are aligned with the costs of inspection activities, which could enable fee adjustments to reduce reliance on general fund appropriations, Congress may wish to require the Secretary of Homeland Security to direct ICE and CBP to establish a regular schedule to review and coordinate on the costs of their respective air passenger immigration inspection activities, and revise the proportion of the fee received by each agency accordingly.	○
2012	**Domestic Disaster Assistance** (Area 51): The Federal Emergency Management Agency (FEMA) could reduce the costs to the federal government related to major disasters declared by the President by updating the principal indicator on which disaster funding decisions are based and better measuring a state's capacity to respond without federal assistance.	○
	Action 1: The FEMA Administrator should re-examine the basis for the Public Assistance per capita indicator and determine whether it accurately reflects a state's capacity to respond to and recover from a disaster without federal assistance. This action was revised to consolidate the three actions cited in GAO's February 2012 report into one action as a result of GAO's September 2012 report, Federal Disaster Assistance: Improved Criteria Needed to Assess a Jurisdiction's Capability to Respond and Recover on Its Own (GAO-12-838). Specifically, in that report GAO recommended that to increase the efficiency and effectiveness of the process for disaster declarations, the Administrator of FEMA should develop and implement a methodology that provides a more comprehensive assessment of a jurisdiction's capability to respond to and recover from a disaster without federal assistance. Providing a more comprehensive assessment of a jurisdiction's capability to respond to and recover from a disaster without federal assistance to support disaster declaration decisions could save billions of dollars. This should include one or more measures of a jurisdiction's fiscal capacity, such as Total Taxable Resources, and consideration of the jurisdiction's response and recovery capabilities. If FEMA continues to use the Public Assistance per capita indicator to assist in identifying a jurisdiction's capabilities to respond to and recover from a disaster, it should adjust the indicator to accurately reflect the annual changes in the U.S. economy since 1986, when the current indicator was first adopted for use. In addition, implementing the adjustment by raising the indicator in steps over several years would give jurisdictions more time to plan for and adjust to the change.	○

**Appendix I: Areas and Actions Identified in
2011-2013 Annual Reports Related to the
Department of Homeland Security**

Annual report	Areas identified	Assessment
2013	**Agricultural Quarantine Inspection Fees** (Area 18): The United States Department of Agriculture's Animal and Plant Health Inspection Service could have achieved as much as $325 million in savings (based on fiscal year 2011 data, as reported in GAO's March 2013 report) by more fully aligning fees with program costs; although the savings would be recurring, the amount would depend on the cost-collections gap in a given fiscal year and would result in a reduced reliance on U.S. Customs and Border Protection's annual Salaries and Expenses appropriations used for agricultural inspection services.	a
	Action 2: The Secretary of Homeland Security should direct CBP to update and widely disseminate guidance to ensure that all ports of entry correctly charge time spent on agriculture-related functions.	a
	Action 3: The Secretaries of Agriculture and Homeland Security should work together to amend overtime regulations for agriculture services so that reimbursable overtime rates are aligned with the costs of those services.	a
	Action 4: The Secretaries of Agriculture and Homeland Security should ensure that all inspection fees are collected when due, including fees for agriculture overtime services that are eligible for reimbursement.	a
2013	**Checked Baggage Screening** (Area 28): By reviewing the appropriateness of the federal cost share the Transportation Security Administration applies to agreements financing airport facility modification projects related to the installation of checked baggage screening systems, the Transportation Security Administration could, if a reduced cost share was deemed appropriate, achieve cost efficiencies of up to $300 million by 2030 and be positioned to install a greater number of optimal baggage screening systems than it currently anticipates.	a
	Action 1: Congress may wish to consider directing TSA to study, in consultation with relevant industry stakeholders, whether the 90 percent federal cost share that TSA generally applies to cost sharing agreements for eligible airport facility modification projects related to the installation of checked baggage screening systems is appropriate or should be adjusted.	a
	Action 2: Congress may wish to consider whether an amendment to current legislation, or enactment of new legislation, is necessary and warranted if it is determined that a change in the current federal cost share that TSA generally applies to these cost sharing agreements is appropriate.	a
2013	**Cloud Computing** (Area 29): Better planning of cloud-based computing solutions provides an opportunity for potential savings of millions of dollars.	a
	Action 1: The Secretaries of Agriculture, Health and Human Services, Homeland Security, State, and the Treasury and the Administrators of the General Services Administration and the Small Business Administration should direct their respective Chief Information Officers to establish estimated costs, performance goals, and plans to retire associated legacy systems for each cloud-based service discussed in the report, as applicable.	a
	Action 2: The Secretaries of Agriculture, Health and Human Services, Homeland Security, State, and the Treasury and the Administrators of the General Services Administration and the Small Business Administration should direct their respective Chief Information Officers to develop, at a minimum, estimated costs, milestones, performance goals, and plans for retiring legacy systems, as applicable, for planned additional cloud-based services.	a
2013	**Information Technology Operations and Maintenance** (Area 30): Strengthening oversight of key federal agencies' major information technology investments in operations and maintenance provides opportunity for savings on billions in information technology investments.	a
	Action 1: The Secretaries of Defense, Homeland Security, Health and Human Services, Veterans Affairs, and the Treasury should direct appropriate officials to annually perform operational analyses on all investments and ensure the assessments include all key factors.	a

Legend:

**Appendix I: Areas and Actions Identified in
2011-2013 Annual Reports Related to the
Department of Homeland Security**

● = Addressed, meaning all actions needed in that area were addressed.

◖ = Partially addressed, meaning at least one action needed in that area showed some progress toward implementation, but not all actions were addressed.

○ = Not addressed, meaning none of the actions needed in that area were addressed.

Source: GAO.

[a]As of April 26, 2013, we have not assessed the 2013 areas identified.

GAO's Mission	The Government Accountability Office, the audit, evaluation, and investigative arm of Congress, exists to support Congress in meeting its constitutional responsibilities and to help improve the performance and accountability of the federal government for the American people. GAO examines the use of public funds; evaluates federal programs and policies; and provides analyses, recommendations, and other assistance to help Congress make informed oversight, policy, and funding decisions. GAO's commitment to good government is reflected in its core values of accountability, integrity, and reliability.
Obtaining Copies of GAO Reports and Testimony	The fastest and easiest way to obtain copies of GAO documents at no cost is through GAO's website (http://www.gao.gov). Each weekday afternoon, GAO posts on its website newly released reports, testimony, and correspondence. To have GAO e-mail you a list of newly posted products, go to http://www.gao.gov and select "E-mail Updates."
Order by Phone	The price of each GAO publication reflects GAO's actual cost of production and distribution and depends on the number of pages in the publication and whether the publication is printed in color or black and white. Pricing and ordering information is posted on GAO's website, http://www.gao.gov/ordering.htm.
	Place orders by calling (202) 512-6000, toll free (866) 801-7077, or TDD (202) 512-2537.
	Orders may be paid for using American Express, Discover Card, MasterCard, Visa, check, or money order. Call for additional information.
Connect with GAO	Connect with GAO on Facebook, Flickr, Twitter, and YouTube. Subscribe to our RSS Feeds or E-mail Updates. Listen to our Podcasts. Visit GAO on the web at www.gao.gov.
To Report Fraud, Waste, and Abuse in Federal Programs	Contact: Website: http://www.gao.gov/fraudnet/fraudnet.htm E-mail: fraudnet@gao.gov Automated answering system: (800) 424-5454 or (202) 512-7470
Congressional Relations	Katherine Siggerud, Managing Director, siggerudk@gao.gov, (202) 512-4400, U.S. Government Accountability Office, 441 G Street NW, Room 7125, Washington, DC 20548
Public Affairs	Chuck Young, Managing Director, youngc1@gao.gov, (202) 512-4800 U.S. Government Accountability Office, 441 G Street NW, Room 7149 Washington, DC 20548

Please Print on Recycled Paper.